The Pain Pill

By Dr. Robert L. Evans III
PhD, LCPC, LPC, MAC, NCC

Copyright 2020 Robert L. Evans All right reserved.

This book or parts thereof may not be reproduced in any form, stored in any retrieval system, or transmitted in any form by any means — electronic, mechanical, photocopy, recording, or otherwise — without prior written permission of the publisher, except as provided by United States of America copyright law. For permission requests, write to the publisher, at admin@empowertoday.net.

For further information visit the author's website at www.empowertoday.net

Pain

If you cannot be honest with yourself, you will not be honest with others. You are a walking contradiction as long as you have not faced your demons. This is your opportunity to search your soul! Find your pain and run towards it!

This process is extremely therapeutic and for some, you may need the assistance of a professional to help you navigate this journey. I highly recommend establishing a solid support system. Also, it is a good idea to prepare your intimate relationships for your journey. Let them know you are going through a metamorphosis. You will be shedding old ways of thinking and behaving. In the end, you will be a new and improved version of yourself!

Introduction

It is not enough to simply know. Knowledge without the courage to exercise it is worthless. This process is worthless because if you don't do anything with your knowledge, it will go with you to the grave when you die! Not exercising your knowledge is like stockpiling a bunch of money and dying prior to doing something remarkable with it!

Some people are collectors of information. They don't have a problem gathering data and becoming experts in knowing how to do things. They keep the information in their back pocket or speak on it very passionately in discussions, but when it comes to execution, they are missing in action. In life we are either *Get 'er doners* or we watch others get it done!

If you finished reading *Run to the Pain*, lose the excuses, because now you know! And obviously, you plan to get it done because you picked up *The Pain Pill*. At this point, it's all about how you move forward from here! See yourself as a Get 'er doner! Answer the questions in this book! Execute the steps you record! Do the work and watch the results!

Get it done!

- What physical pain are you ignoring? And Why? After answering these questions, list the steps you plan to take to resolve the pain? If you need to schedule appointments, write them down and track your progress to resolve the injury.

- Who are you meeting with for your appointment(s)? & List the date(s) for the appointment(s)?

- When was the last time you had a physical Exam? Are you following the recommendations? If you are not complying with the recommendations, Why? If you need to schedule an exam, write it down and track the progress. If finances/insurance is in the way of your exam, write down your steps to resolve the issue then follow the previous steps.

_____
_____
_____
_____
_____
_____
_____
_____
_____
_____
_____
_____
_____
_____
_____
_____
_____

- How do you allow emotional pain to operate in your life? Review the list below and if any of these issues applies to you, write down specifically how it applies and then write down your strategy to remedy this issue in your life. If you do not have a strategy, that means you will need assistance with developing one, so write down your steps to find someone who you will contact for help.

    - Power and *control issues*
    - Broken and *unresolved relationships*
    - Lack of ability to build or sustain *trust* within relationships
    - Lack of *passion for life*
    - Lack of interest in *pursuing dreams*
    - Lack of interest in developing *gifts and talents*
    - Lack of ability to effectively *regulate emotions*
    - Lack of *self-fulfillment*
    - Lack of *self-efficacy*
    - Lack of *self-esteem*
    - Lack of ability to be *vulnerable*
    - Lack of ability and/or desire to *love*
    - Lack of desire to *build a family*
    - Lack of desire to be in *a monogamous relationship*

_____

_____

_____

_____

_____

- Is there anything you are not pursuing because of someone else's opinion? If so, write it down and the write down your steps to pursue that dream if you determine it is in your best interest.

- How is fear operating in your life? Is it a Freezer or a Fire? Are you allowing fear to freeze you in your tracks, or is it operating like a fire under your bottom, giving you the motivation to put one foot in front of the other? If you want to move from freezer to fire, what steps are you going to take to change how fear operates in your life?

    Remember, Discomfort + Vision = Motivation.

_____

_____

_____

_____

_____

_____

_____

_____

_____

_____

_____

_____

_____

_____

_____

- List the things in your life that are so uncomfortable you wish you could change them.

_____
_____
_____
_____
_____
_____
_____
_____
_____
_____
_____
_____
_____
_____
_____
_____
_____
_____
_____

- Identify your alternate vision for those uncomfortable things you listed above.

- List the objects in the way of you making your vision a reality. These are the barriers you must have the courage to face and overcome. Courage is not the absence of the fear. It is the presence of action amidst fear.

_____
_____
_____
_____
_____
_____
_____
_____
_____
_____
_____
_____
_____
_____
_____
_____
_____
_____
_____

Conditioning

The main ingredient to becoming an outstanding therapist is Self-Awareness. You can learn strategies, you can go to school and experience the best training from the most elite educators, but if you are unaware of who you are, your effectiveness will be crippled.

You must know your biases, your aches, your wounds, and you must actively pursue correction and healing. In fact, the journey to become aware of one's self, is essential to our purpose as human beings. If you have not done so, this is your opportunity for self-exploration!

Once you are self-aware, identify your desire and then become intentional about achieving it!

- What are the contributing factors to who you are? List all of the things about you that you view as negative and also list the things that others view about you as negative.

_____
_____
_____
_____
_____
_____
_____
_____
_____
_____
_____
_____
_____
_____
_____
_____
_____
_____
_____
_____

- Identify the negative things on your list that you desire to change.

_____
_____
_____
_____
_____
_____
_____
_____
_____
_____
_____
_____
_____
_____
_____
_____
_____
_____
_____
_____

- Write down your strategic plan to correct those things that you desire to change. Remember, just because we have been one way, it doesn't mean we have to continue to be that way. Don't be satisfied with mediocrity.

- Write down the positive things about yourself that both you recognize and that others recognize. Once you have identified the positive things about yourself, write this list in plain view someplace where you can see it regularly. Every morning, start your day by reminding yourself of how awesome you are by verbalizing the positive attributes you have identified.

_____

_____

_____

_____

_____

_____

_____

_____

_____

_____

_____

_____

_____

_____

_____

- What positive character traits do you desire to add to your list?

- What is your strategic plan to add those desired character traits to your daily way of living?

- How do you manage anger? If you manage it poorly, what steps do you plan to take to improve your anger-management skills?

- How do you recover from failure? Do you quit or keep trying?

- List anything that you failed to complete, but still wish to finish. Then list your plan to complete those identified tasks.

Adversity

Adversity is woven into the fabric of our very existence. It is designed to expose our weaknesses so that we can make corrections and become stronger. We must embrace this fact and look forward to it. Running away from our problems stunts our growth. We must identify the adversity we are facing so that we can overcome it! We cannot bury or ignore it! It will only become more difficult to conquer later. Run to it! And give it the good ol' Dwayne Johnson "Smack Down!"

- What waves of adversity are hitting you at this moment?

- How are you handling them? Are you running away or throwing your shoulder into the wave(s)? List each wave and identify if you are running away from it or throwing your shoulder into it.

- What perceived barriers are in the way of you throwing your shoulder into the wave(s) you identified above?

- List the factors that make you confident about facing the particular waves you are throwing your shoulder into. **You may need to duplicate those same factors for the waves you are running away from. For example, if you have resources to assist with one wave, you may need to build similar resources to assist with the more challenging waves.**

_____
_____
_____
_____
_____
_____
_____
_____
_____
_____
_____
_____
_____
_____
_____
_____

- List a specific plan of attack to address all of the waves you are currently experiencing. (Identify at least one person and all of the resources necessary to assist you with your quest to overcome these waves)

Lessons Learned

What good is experiencing extremely uncomfortable and painful situations, if we do not learn from them? Unless you are sadistic, your reaction to a painful situation should be to find ways to avoid a repeat occurrence of that event. Don't just keep the lessons in your head! Write them down! This is your blueprint for success! This can be the start to something great that you can pass down to your children, mentees, or students.

You may have all the best intentions and desire to do better because you experienced something tragic and learned from it; but if you cannot remember the details of the lesson, you will experience reiteration of loss. Wouldn't it be convenient to remember the steps you learned?

- List all of the failures you have learned from. Write down the important lessons you learned from each identified failure.

Running to the Pain

I often hear people rebut the idea of forgiveness because they associate it with weakness. Some people believe that forgiveness is a failure in accountability. So, they maintain an open wound, with the expectation that their exposed pain will result in the purification of someone else's imperfection. It's as if I decided to allow my broken arm to stay broken with the expectation that my friend's attitude will change as a result. Does that make any sense? Instead, two mutually exclusive activities must take place. I must tend to my broken arm, and my friend must do the work to improve his attitude.

Forgiveness is the key to your healing. It allows you to release the burden of harbored negative emotions so that you can be free to experience love and happiness. Remember, you can forgive a person and hold them accountable at the same time. For example, you can forgive a person yet block them from your social media pages. You do not have to maintain a relationship with a poisonous person. Forgive and let them go!

- Who have you not forgiven? Identify if you are going to forgive them to let them go or to maintain a relationship with them.

_____

_____

_____

_____

_____

_____

_____

_____

_____

_____

_____

_____

_____

_____

_____

_____

_____

_____

_____

- **Who is truly to blame for your pain?** List the events in your life that are still painful to think about and identify who is to blame for the outcomes for those events. **Are you alone** to blame? **Is it someone else? If so, identify the person or entity. Or are both you and someone else to blame for your pain? Be specific in your identification**

_____
_____
_____
_____
_____
_____
_____
_____
_____
_____
_____
_____
_____
_____
_____
_____

For those events you blame yourself for, follow these steps to forgive yourself for each event. *Acknowledge, Make Amends* and *Make Corrections*

- **Make Amends:** If you listed events above that you have taken responsibility for, then you have already acknowledge your personal role in your pain. List below each event and the name of any person(s) who you falsely accused for your pain. Once you have reached out to them and apologized for your behavior, give yourself credit next to each event you listed by writing down "Mission Accomplished".

_____

_____

_____

_____

_____

_____

_____

_____

_____

_____

_____

_____

_____

- **Make Corrections:** Write down the events that you forgive yourself for, and next to each entry, write down the lessons you learned and the corrections you will make so that you do not inflict the same pain upon yourself in the future.

_____
_____
_____
_____
_____
_____
_____
_____
_____
_____
_____
_____
_____
_____
_____
_____
_____

For those events you blame God for, follow the steps to forgive God for each event. *Seek, Listen, and Be Ready.*

- **Seek:** Write down the events that you forgive God for, and next to them write down the specific timeframe you will assign to prayer and fasting. Also write down the time of day you will assign to praying. This is your special time for speaking with your source. Identify a different item you will fast from for each event. Each item you choose needs to be significant in your life and daily activities.

_____

_____

_____

_____

_____

_____

_____

_____

_____

_____

_____

_____

_____

- **Listen:** Write down the events that you are forgiving God for, and next to them write down the specific time of day you will reserve for meditation. Your timeframe for meditation should coincide with the timeframe for prayer, whether 30 days, 60 days, or another specified length of time.

- What pain/malice are you holding onto? Write it down, along with how the negativity in your heart is playing out in your life? For instance, Are you unable to make or keep friendships? Are you estranged from your family? Are you afraid to love again? Did you give up on men or women as a result of past hurt?

_____

_____

_____

_____

_____

_____

_____

_____

_____

_____

_____

_____

_____

_____

_____

- List the pros and cons of any troublesome relationship that is still in your life. If the negatives consume the positives, why are you maintaining this relationship? Write it down. If you realize you need to end a relationship, write down how and when you plan to do it. Give yourself a benchmark.

_____
_____
_____
_____
_____
_____
_____
_____
_____
_____
_____
_____
_____
_____
_____
_____
_____

- What is your pride in the way of? List the items. How will you defeat your pride? What's taking you so long to *Decide* to *Accept* your power and overcome the obstacle that pride is blocking you from hurdling?

- What do you need to let go? List it along with the steps you will take to let it go? If you don't know the steps, identify who you will reach out to for help in letting go.

_____

_____

_____

_____

_____

_____

_____

_____

_____

_____

_____

_____

_____

_____

_____

_____

_____

- Who is in your support network? You should have support in all areas of your life where you are lacking. If you are not an electrician, you should contact one before trying to do major electrical work. If you do not have a support network to assist you with the areas of your life where there is struggle, write down your steps to build and/or expand your network.

Medication

Some people do not like the idea of taking medication. They think medication is an indication that something is wrong. The truth is, sometimes it is and other times it's not. We are always taking medication, whether we realize it or not. When we have a scoop of that favorite ice-cream. When we watch our favorite comedian, who has us crying while laughing. When we kiss our loved one and feel that chill down the back of our neck. When we exercise and feel a sense of release afterwards. These are all forms of self-medication. It doesn't have to be a pill we swallow and digest.

If you completed the exercises in this book, you have been taking medication. Don't stop there! These questions provided you an opportunity to learn and exercise coping strategies that should become a part of your daily activities.

You started out as a caterpillar, and after identifying who you have been and who you desire to be, you have the blessed opportunity to emerge as a butterfly! This means a lifestyle change! So, continue to identify your limitations by welcoming adversity and take the necessary steps to improve! Forgive! Avoid complacency, fear, and distorted thinking! Become intentional! And don't walk! Run to the Pain!

www.ingramcontent.com/pod-product-compliance
Lightning Source LLC
Chambersburg PA
CBHW030915080526
44589CB00010B/308